At seven miles wide and seven miles long, San Francisco is best understood by those who (mostly) hoof it. So though we're both locals, photographer Meghan and I hit the pavement to explore the city and all its enclaves to bring you the finest bars, eateries, sights and shops to be found. The best moments came when we took a wrong turn and accidentally walked into a gem. While Meghan _____ I would chat with the store owner who might _____ er friend's jewelry shop _____ stro a few blocks away, wh _____ t went, like

Our favorites in _____ co's west Coast style, love of the _____ adventurous appetite. Use our picks as starting points, but let your curiosity guide you. If you get lost and accidentally wander into tourist central, allow us, through this guide, to get you back on course.

---

meghan caudill
photographer

Meghan Caudill is a freelance photographer and designer now living in San Francisco's NoPa neighborhood. She grew up in the South but fell in love with San Francisco when she moved here three years ago. Since new places pop up so often, she continues to enjoy exploring the city by bike or on foot. When she's not behind the lens of her camera, you can find her tackling DIY projects, trying new recipes or searching for the best burger in SF.

lauren ladoceour
editor

A lover of bourbon and bonfires, Lauren Ladoceour is a food and lifestyle writer based in San Francisco's Mission. Her job is mostly to hang out with chefs and bartenders and then write about it for magazines such as *Food Arts*, *San Francisco* and *Yoga Journal*. But come Saturday, she's working on her biannual *Weekend Almanac*. She fully believes life happens Friday through Sunday, and the best way to experience it is to get out of the house and try something new.

where to lay your weary head

Rest up, relax and recharge

HOTEL ZETTA

A shopper's haven near Union Square

55 5th Street / (+1) 415 543 8555 / viceroyhotelgroup.com/zetta

Standard double from $269

Hotel Zetta is San Francisco's newest place for overnighters to rest their weary heads, and it combines everything I love about boutique hotels with a luxe design aesthetic. Downstairs you've got an awesome bar and restaurant serving classic English fare and a sleek lounge that draws in sharply dressed 9-to-5ers for a post-work drink. If you're in town to do some shopping, you can't beat the location either: Union Square and two malls are all less than two blocks away.

INN AT THE PRESIDIO

Peace and quiet in the city's national park

42 Moraga Avenue / (+1) 415 800 7356 / innatthepresidio.com

Standard queen from $215

Enjoy a quiet respite in this peaceful hideaway that was once army officers' quarters. Grab a rocking chair on the porch, or trek down to the nearby beach for a run. Each room has a fireplace and plenty of Georgian Revival charm, making the Inn at the Presidio the perfect place to stay if you need a break from the crowds and want a taste of NorCal nature.

INN AT THE PRESIDIO

THE GOOD HOTEL

An eco-friendly crashpad

112 7th Street / (+1) 415 621 7001 / thegoodhotel.com

Standard double from $89

I love this boutique hotel's young, urban vibe. Platform beds come dressed in sheets made from the finest organic materials, and there are colorful bikes in the lobby that you can borrow when you want to go explore. The rooms are small but well-appointed with nice details, much like the Ace Hotel in Portland, Palm Springs and New York. It's a great deal if you're on a budget. Plus, you're just a short walk to the Civic Center/UN Plaza BART station.

THE PALACE HOTEL

Downtown grandeur

2 Montgomery Street / (+1) 415 512 1111 / sfpalace.com

Standard double from $319

Opulence abounds here, making it an ideal choice if your dream is to stretch out in a classic San Francisco landmark. Modern amenities – such as the gorgeous indoor pool – come laced with Edwardian touches, including a bar with dark booths that will have you screaming for a Manhattan with a Champagne float (a popular cocktail in 1909, when the hotel was re-opened after the 1906 earthquake). More 21st-century finds are just five minutes away at the Jewish Contemporary Museum and Yerba Buena Center for the Arts.

THE PARKER GUEST HOUSE

Comfort on Dolores Park

520 Church Street / (+1) 888 520 7275 / parkerguesthouse.com

Economy queen from $169

If you plan on spending most of your time in the Mission or the Castro, check into The Parker Guest House, which sits on the border of the two neighborhoods best known for their nightlife and restaurants. It's a clean, modern bed-and-breakfast with steam rooms, sherry service and a sunny backyard garden. Bring earplugs if you're a light sleeper, though – the J Muni train runs past this yellow B&B until midnight.

north beach

barbary coast, financial district, embarcadero

———◆———

You know all those movies shot in San Francisco? Lots of them were filmed in the northeast of the city, a historic area along the original Gold Rush coastline. Most notable among them is North Beach, with its Beat Generation and Italian roots. The Embarcadero is gorgeous for its bayside location and the Ferry Building. A few famous car chases were filmed in the Financial District, while Russian Hill, with its charming cable cars and tree-lined streets, is where the impossibly cool Steve McQueen showed off his driving prowess in *Bullitt*.

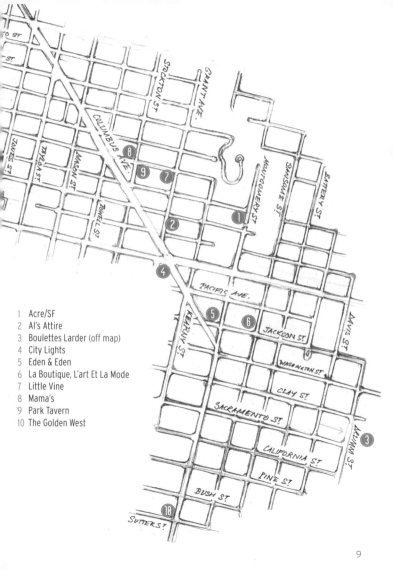

1 Acre/SF
2 Al's Attire
3 Boulettes Larder (off map)
4 City Lights
5 Eden & Eden
6 La Boutique, L'art Et La Mode
7 Little Vine
8 Mama's
9 Park Tavern
10 The Golden West

ACRE/SF

Casual finery and great coffee

301 Union Street / (+1) 415 875 9590 / acresf.com / Closed Tuesday

I'm not going to lie and tell you Acre/SF is easy to get to. You have to climb
three blocks of serious hill to reach the boutique, which teeters at the very
tippy top of Union Street, just below Coit Tower. But the hike is well worth
it. The boutique used to be a long-standing Italian delicatessen but all
that's left of that now is an old magazine stand and shopping cart. Though
there's still plenty to snack on while you shop. Once you enter, order a Blue
Bottle drip coffee and a pastry, and take in the view before getting to the
clothes. If you love the black-and-white look, you'll die and go to heaven. No
need to take a special shopping trip to New York's SoHo when you've got all
the Alexander Wang you could want right here in the nosebleed section.

AL'S ATTIRE

Custom-made clothing and shoes

1300 Grant Avenue / (+1) 415 693 9900 / alsattire.com / Open daily

Every time a good friend of mine returns from visiting his family in Genoa, where the men wear chicly tailored everything, he's ready to trade his sweatpants for a custom-made wardrobe. So he goes to Al Ribaya of Al's Attire, to make him perfect-fitting linen pants, skinny trousers and sharp blazers. Al's has hundreds of vintage design cards, everything from heirloom fabric to American-made denim, and a rad collection of antique buttons. The clothes are all very bespoke Americana (representing 1940-something to 1970-something), with a shoe rack to match. As for my friend, he plays a finely dressed Michael Corleone for a few weeks and then slips back into sweats.

BOULETTES LARDER

Farm-fresh fare and pantry

1 Ferry Building Marketplace / **(+1) 415 399 1155** / **bouletteslarder.com**
Closed Monday

The Ferry Building used to be a quaint place where I'd wander the stalls and sample cheeses and olive oils. Now it welcomes thousands of visitors with fine palates every day. Though there remains one quiet nook in the form of Boulettes Larder. The pine nuts for sale in this store within a restaurant are famous in these parts, but grab a quarter pounder or the vegetarian farmhouse lunch if you fancy something more substantial. Sitting by the roaring fire is a cozy reprieve from the strollers and gourmet tours taking place just outside and it's all capped off with an excellent view of the Bay Bridge.

CITY LIGHTS

Supporting local writing talent

261 Columbus Avenue / (+1) 415 362 8193 / citylights.com / Open daily

For all those naysayers who say print is dead, I point you to Lawrence Ferlinghetti's City Lights bookstore. Throughout the week, the city's It writers (poets, journalists, novelists, short-story authors) can be seen here, browsing or giving a reading among the aisles of rare lit mags, bestsellers and titles the bookstore has published. This space has long fostered local young writing talent, perhaps most famously Allen Ginsberg and Jack Kerouac. So I tell people: come for the history and romanticism of the Beat Generation, or come to see the next great voice of this generation. Just leave your Kindle at home.

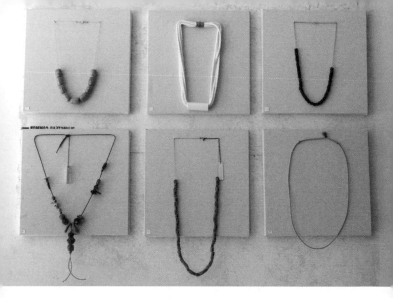

EDEN & EDEN

English motifs for your mood board

560 Jackson Street / (+1) 415 983 0490 / edenandeden.com
Closed Sunday

For years, I walked straight past Eden & Eden on the way to a favorite coffee shop until one day a tribal necklace in the window caught my eye. Inside this spare but eclectic boutique, I found so much more, including a lot of hot designers and crafts from the owner's native England. I adored the wool teapot cozies made here in San Francisco and the billowy jackets that had a bit of Elizabethan flare. Now I go inside every few weeks to check out all the new goods and chat with the owner about her latest finds and the cool stories behind them.

LA BOUTIQUE, L'ART ET LA MODE

European style for your closet and home

414 Jackson Street / (+1) 415 693 9950 / laboutique-galerie.com
Closed Sunday

In a spacious gallery with a sunny loft, La Boutique is part fashion, part art mecca. Downstairs, the style of the womenswear hanging on the spare clothing racks is edgy but elegant and splashed with plenty of black, making the designer looks comparable to anything you'd find in Paris' Le Marais neighborhood. Upstairs, you've got a mix of emerging artists and mid-century antiques for the home. When I'm in Jackson Square working, I like to take my lunch break here, combing through the treasures and remembering my visits to my favorite Parisian corner, where dressing up is an everyday affair.

LITTLE VINE

A taste of Wine Country

**1541 Grant Avenue / (+1) 415 738 2221 / shoplittlevine.com
Closed Monday**

There are restaurants aplenty in this European nook of North Beach, but high-quality markets, the kind where you can pop in for a good wine and crusty bread to go with a hunk of artisanal cheese, are hard to come by. Little Vine is a bona fide neighborhood corner market, which just happens to make killer sandwiches and stock everything you just ran out of. Every once in a while, a visiting winemaker will stop by and set up a free tasting. Last time, I sipped a lovely Sauvignon Blanc from the Sierras while waiting for a small picnic and half bottle to go.

MAMA'S

Down-home eggs and stacks

1701 Stockton Street / (+1) 415 362 6421 / mamas-sf.com
Closed Monday

Mama's is an all-American family restaurant that stands out in the neighborhood's sea of Italian pizzerias and noodle joints. This little corner diner and bakery is drenched in what can only be described as classic country cute, it reminds me of all those homey kitchens with checkered curtains in 1980s U.S. sitcoms. Anyway, it's not the décor that's the draw, it's the stacks of pancakes and French toast. My choice? Mama's Monte Cristo, cut into four triangles for easy dunking in raspberry jam, just like mom used to make. Before you can claim a seat, you'll need to stand in line like everyone else, but by the time you finish at the register, a table will be cleared and ready for you. Guaranteed.

PARK TAVERN

Stylish American in an Italian heartland

1652 Stockton Street / (+1) 415 989 7300 / parktavernsf.com
Open daily

When restaurateurs Jennifer Puccio and Anna Weinberg took over this large space, they went for something upscale with a dark and moody tavern look but kept things casual enough for patrons to feel comfy at the bar with a Negroni and one of Jennifer's burgers, made famous at her other restaurant, Marlowe. For a relative newcomer in North Beach, it feels very grand and established. It already has a signature item on the menu: creamy deviled eggs spiced with jalapeño and thick-cut bacon. My enjoyment of them must have been obvious: as I ate, six diners came up to me and asked what I was having before ordering a plate themselves.

THE GOLDEN WEST

A secret alleyway takeout window

8 Trinity Alley / (+1) 415 216 6443 / theauwest.com
Closed Saturday and Sunday

Fine-dining chef Dennis Leary is very concerned with size. He likes his sandwiches not too big and his restaurants itty bitty. The Golden West is really just a takeout that caters to the 9-to-5 crowds who either eat curbside or carry their market-fresh sandwich and seasonal salad back to their desks. But this little window (cleverly marked "Au") is a lifesaver if you're in the financial district, an area awash with watery tomatoes and wilted lettuce. The lunch specials here change daily, so if you're wondering what's on the menu, check out their Twitter feed.

offshore fun

Water sports, from mild to wild

Between the America's Cup, fishing and shipping industries, the Bay Area loves its surrounding waters. Fog or shine, the **ferry to Angel Island** is a lovely way to get out on the bay and have a picnic on this forested island between Alcatraz and Tiburon in the North Bay. From here, you get views of the city, but avoid going on the weekends when the island can be crowded with urban dwellers desperate for some nature. (There's also a small restaurant, bar and museum for when everyone's had their fill of the outdoors.) Outside of the winter months, the island is open to overnight campers who don't mind high winds and have forward planned and reserved a permit weeks ahead of time.

But I'm not the best planner, and sometimes I'm dying for sun. So I'll get on BART and take it east until I hit July weather at **Lake Merritt** in the East Bay. Sure, it's a manmade lake, but it's a nice respite and a quick shot of vitamin D. Rent a canoe or sailboat at the boathouse, and after stop by the Lake Chalet for a beer and sweet potato fries waterside.

Back in the city during baseball season, I'll venture out to **City Kayak** near McCovey Cove to try and catch balls that clear AT&T Park's walls. But the real water babies can be found most mornings at **The Dolphin Club** near the Marina. Swimmers of all stripes suit up and do laps in the protected cove to prepare for triathlons or just get the blood pumping first thing before work. Join them if you dare!

CITY KAYAK
Pier 40, (+1) 415 294 1050, citykayak.com
open Friday to Monday

FERRY TO ANGEL ISLAND
Pier 39, (+1) 415 705 8200, blueandgoldfleet.com, open daily

LAKE MERRITT BOATING CENTER
568 Bellevue Avenue (Oakland), (+1) 510 238 2196
open Saturday and Sunday

THE DOLPHIN CLUB
502 Jefferson Street, (+1) 415 441 9329, dolphinclub.org,
closed Sunday and Monday

south of market

south beach, dogpatch, potrero hill, bayview

Want to know where the up-and-coming places are? Follow the weekday morning coffee lines that begin south of Market Street and east of Van Ness. South of Market (SoMa) and South Beach are tech central, a virtual office park that's packed with people Monday through Friday and then pretty sleepy come the weekend. Some of the tech scene spills over into Dogpatch along the waterfront, which has been getting an influx of new restaurants and businesses among the old warehouses. The new light rail runs through this sunny neighborhood, and shops and cafés are appearing as people are moving in. Bayview still has a largely industrial feel, but there are some gems worth seeking out if you're over this way. Above the waterfront is Potrero Hill, the warmest neighborhood in town. It's largely residential and much more quaint than Bayview, and its restaurants are some of SF's best-kept secrets.

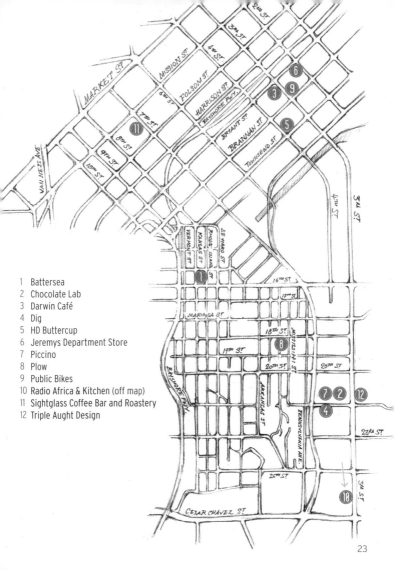

1 Battersea
2 Chocolate Lab
3 Darwin Café
4 Dig
5 HD Buttercup
6 Jeremys Department Store
7 Piccino
8 Plow
9 Public Bikes
10 Radio Africa & Kitchen (off map)
11 Sightglass Coffee Bar and Roastery
12 Triple Aught Design

23

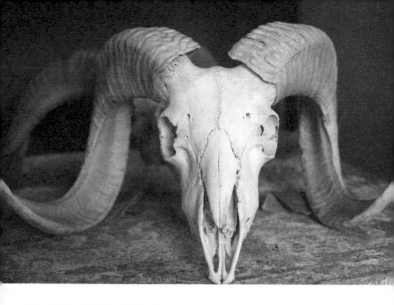

BATTERSEA

Industrial antiques with panache

297 Kansas Street / (+1) 415 553 8500 / batterseasf.com
Closed Saturday and Sunday

The cool-gray interior of globe-trotter Will Wick's Battersea is a nice respite on those rare hot days when the fog lifts and the sun beats down. Will's got a really good thing going for him, namely his ability to repurpose furniture as well as small, industrial (and sometimes nautical) antiquities. It's the kind of thing I would do if I had the patience to comb through flea markets and the discipline to finish any of my DIY projects. Each time I visit the 1,200-square-foot space I always find tons of new stock. With no two pieces alike, you've got to wonder if Will's imagination is endless.

CHOCOLATE LAB

A little savory to go with your sweet

**801 22nd Street / (+1) 415 489 2881 / chocolatelabsf.com
Closed Monday**

Michael Recchiuti is the man behind some of the most decadent chocolate bars in SF. But the items at his offshoot Chocolate Lab café are more savory than sweet: fluffy soufflés, cranberry bean and tomato salad, open-faced sandwiches topped with bay shrimp and creme fraîche. I always save room for dessert, which showcases Michael's background as a pastry chef. If you don't have time for a proper meal, he's got an impressive takeaway menu full of fresh tartines. It's also the best place for a civilized happy hour with homemade chicken liver pâté finished with strawberry balsamic *marmellata* (jam), cornichons and toast points.

DARWIN CAFE

Cozy, casual dishes worth the wait

212 Ritch Street / (+1) 415 800 8668 / darwincafesf.com
Closed Saturday and Sunday

You've heard of techies made famous — and rich — for developing apps like Instagram and social networks a la Twitter. The birthplaces of many of those start-ups are around Darwin Café, a pocket-sized restaurant with the best lunch in the neighborhood. See, most cafés around here cater a dorm-room diet of burritos and burgers but Darwin is more refined. Think colorful kale salads and fresh baguette sandwiches like you'd find in Paris. If you can snag one of the few tables, you might just see the next IPO millionaire bouncing ideas off a back-end engineer. Come Friday night, though, Darwin and the rest of this corner of SoMa empty out until Monday morning when the techies return to work on the next big thing.

DIG

Old World wines

**1005 Minnesota Street / (+1) 415 648 6133 / digwinesf.com
Closed Sunday and Monday**

A lot of juice heads come to the Bay Area for its proximity to Napa,
Sonoma and Anderson Valley vineyards. Lately, small production wine
producers have been setting up shop inside the city's somewhat
gritty Dogpatch neighborhood and converting the empty warehouses
into vino-sipping destinations. But for a taste of something rare and
international, let Wayne Garcia guide you through his favorite Italian and
French vintage bottles inside his wine merchant shop. He'll even suggest
favorable food pairings and seek out older labels upon request. Now
that's good bottle service.

HD BUTTERCUP

Bold furniture styles from every decade

290 Townsend Street / **(+1) 415 820 4788** / **hdbuttercup.com**
Open daily

Furniture shopping in San Francisco usually comes in a trifecta of varieties: consignment vintage, box stores or boutiques. Problem is you have to run over town to hit all three. But at HD Buttercup (a transplant from SoCal), you get the best of all worlds in two stories and what feels like 30,000 square feet of showroom. The first floor has everything from shabby chic to Anglophile designs. Upstairs is a healthy dose of *Mad Men*-inspired side tables and accessories. Sound like an interior-designing identity crisis? Maybe. Yet shopping at HD Buttercup means you don't have to be pigeon-holed and that your home can be of a design that's uniquely yours.

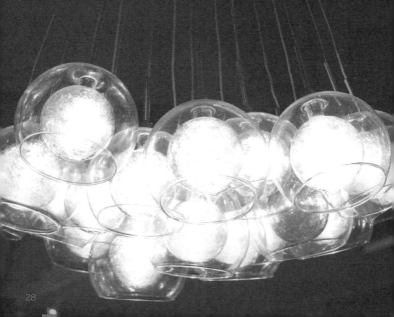

JEREMYS DEPARTMENT STORE

Year-round designer sales

2 South Park / (+1) 415 882 4929 / jeremys.com / Open daily

I'm not really someone who's ever cared a whole lot about labels or department stores, and yet this little South Park gem makes me feel right at home. On the first floor are deeply discounted shoes and higher-end stuff (the shop gets its merchandise from designer sample sales, photo shoots, window displays and customer returns from more traditional department stores). I spent hours trying on gowns that were half the price you'd pay elsewhere. Upstairs you'll discover more casual styles. On my last visit I picked out an edgy The Row dress and a killer pair of low boots that would have bled me dry at Barneys. Score!

PICCINO

Cal-Ital meeting place

1001 Minnesota Street / (+1) 415 824 4224 / piccinocafe.com
Closed Monday

Since 2006, Piccino has served as a kind of meeting ground along the abandoned shipyard waterfront. When it had to move its pasta and pizza operation down the block, customers duly followed. It's now housed in a gleaming yellow Victorian building, a space it shares with a wine bar, tasting room and MAC boutique. When I was there, trying out a nectarine and nettle pizza with burrata (which tasted like late summer in a savory pie), a longtime diner sat down and had her regular order already on its way when the waiter saw her, as though she was one of the family.

PLOW

Grub worth getting out of bed for

1299 18th Street / (+1) 415 821 7569 / eatatplow.com / Closed Monday

Potrero Hill is a quiet family neighborhood but the pancakes at Plow make the hike there worthwhile. The brunch-time lemon ricotta cakes are so popular, they're also on the lunch menu, so on my last visit, I started with a pork sandwich and then finished off with a sweet stack. This is classic diner food done to perfection. Even full, I couldn't help but stare at my neighbor's plate. Golden yellow yolks spilled into a pile of crispy rosemary potatoes. Of course, she was a regular from the neighborhood who told me that the creamy-centered potatoes have a growing cult following of their own.

PUBLIC BIKES

Punchy urban cruisers

123 South Park Avenue / (+1) 415 896 0123 / publicbikes.com
Closed Sunday and Tuesday

Designer Rob Forbes is known locally for his shapely modern furniture
with a mid-century twist. At Public Bikes, his Dutch-inspired cruisers
are equally sleek. His spare showroom sits in the middle of the most
European-looking neighborhood in the city, South Park. I happily took a
few laps around the park to test out the new models and ring a brass bell.
The design is ergonomic, with low-maintenance internal gears that make
for a stylish ride. These bikes are for both beginners and for experienced
cyclists who want to make a fashion statement and accessorize their ride
with panache and classic flair. Flowers and wine for a front-riding basket
sold separately.

RADIO AFRICA & KITCHEN

Soul-warming food

4800 3rd Street / (+1) 415 420 2486 / radioafricakitchen.com
Closed Sunday and Monday

Ethiopian-born Eskender Aseged believes that food should invoke
good memories. Eskender named his restaurant Radio Africa &
Kitchen because of all the times in his hometown when he and his
neighbors would gather around the one radio in his neighborhood to
listen to music and sports, laugh and eat. Now, there are tons of soul
food kitchens in SF's Bayview, most of them indistinguishable from
the other. Not so at Radio Africa & Kitchen, where you won't find any
mundane fried chicken or waffles. Instead, the ever-changing menu
is pulled from several North African cuisines, including Moroccan and
Ethiopian, and is light and seasonal, perfect for sharing.

SIGHTGLASS COFFEE BAR AND ROASTERY

A new wave coffee klatch

270 7th Street / (+1) 415 861 1313 / sightglasscoffee.com / Open daily

Between the booming tech scene and SF's obsession with artisanal ingredients, this town is full of all sorts of nerds: bourbon nerds, food photography nerds and of course coffee nerds. Justin and Jerad Morrison's Sightglass Coffee Bar and Roastery is characterized not so much by the boutique beans sourced from all over the world but by the Slayer espresso machine. Think of it as a manual camera with an amazing amount of settings, which ensures you get an exquisite cup. And in the pastry cabinet, you'll find elegant treats from the city's umpteen bakeries.

TRIPLE AUGHT DESIGN

Army-inspired outdoor gear

660 22nd Street / **(+1) 415 613 1386** / **tripleaughtdesign.com**
Closed Monday

I was walking off a boozy brunch when I stumbled upon Triple Aught Design. Housed in a warehouse with a metal roll-up door, I couldn't tell if it was a store or a storage unit. Once inside, it was clear that this was no garage sale. As well as some serious-looking mannequin busts, all the jackets and army accessories neatly displayed in shadow boxes are perfect for those who loved playing G.I. Joe and Lady Jane as kids and who grew up into stylish men and women who want a parka that's as suited to the mountains as it is to city streets.

the tech trail

Where the start-up crowd works and plays

BLUE BOTTLE COFFEE
66 Mint Street, (+1) 510 653 3394, bluebottlecoffee.com,
open daily

SIGHTGLASS COFFEE BAR AND ROASTERY
270 7th Street, (+1) 415 861 1313, sightglasscoffee.com,
open daily

TECHSHOP
926 Howard Street, (+1) 415 263 9161, techshop.ws, open daily

SAISON
178 Townsend Street, (+1) 415 828 7990, saisonsf.com, closed
Sunday and Monday

SOUTH PARK
Between 2nd and 3rd Streets and Bryant and Brannan
Streets, open daily

In case you didn't know, San Francisco is pretty tech-obsessed. And ground zero of that obsession lies between the CalTrain Station (aka the commuter gateway to Silicon Valley) and South Park, a quaint lawn space where Twitter was first hatched. Surrounding South Park and the train station is the greater SoMa neighborhood, with its luxury lofts and empty-looking warehouses. Don't be fooled though: those warehouses are hives of engineers, designers and founders toiling to create the next big thing, be that an app, a piece of hardware or a social media tool. The neighborhood is also home to Zynga, Yahoo, Square and a bevy of scrappy start-ups. In the morning, you have a good chance of running into an Evan Williams or Marissa Mayer-type getting their java at **Blue Bottle Coffee** near Jack Dorsey's loft in Mint Plaza. Though apparently Dorsey prefers **Sightglass Coffee Bar and Roastery** (see pg 34) closer to the Square offices on Market Street.

At lunch, claim a piece of the grass on **South Park**, along with hundreds of tech workers downing takeout from one of the restaurants encircling the park. Or get a day pass to **TechShop**, an open workspace with a 3-D printer and any other piece of equipment you need to make hardware.

After 6pm, grab drinks and refined small bites at **Saison**'s upscale wood bar and see which IPO-rich founder is eating at the chef's counter tonight. A single meal may set you back a few hundred bucks, but there's no dress code at Saison, probably because it boasts several hoodied tech stars as investors. Talk about knowing your audience.

mission

valencia corridor, mission creek, 24th street corridor

The two corridors and Mission Creek anchor what's collectively called the Mission. From 16th to 26th Streets, the Valencia Corridor acts as a kind of hipster runway lined with a slew of restaurants on either side. To the east is Mission Creek, far enough away from the action of Valencia to have a more residential feel, but not for much longer. Established and up-and-coming chefs are starting to open up shop in the small neighborhood, along with galleries and boutique bike shops. To the south is 24th Street Corridor, the last holdout for the area's Latin American roots. It's got all that Valencia offers, along with art, cultural centers and cheap eats.

1 20 SPOT
2 Alite Designs (off map)
3 Bar Tartine
4 Claudia Kussano
5 Dijital Fix
6 Fine Arts Optical
7 Mission Bowling Club
8 Mr. Pollo
9 Salumeria
10 The NWBLK
11 The Voyager Shop
12 Wise Sons

20 SPOT

Wine and small plates

3565 20th Street / (+1) 415 624 3140 / 20spot.com / Closed Tuesday

I love that Bodhi Freedom kept the record store sign out front when he signed the lease to open his wine bar. To be clear, the vino takes center stage here but the menu of small plates is a more than decent support act. Sit at the reclaimed eucalyptus bar to enjoy Old World wines and a relaxed supper. Or come in at the end of the night (20 SPOT is excellent for evening eats) to mingle with the city's star chefs who come for a drink and a bite after work.

ALITE DESIGNS

Camp in style

2505 Mariposa Street / (+1) 415 626 1526 / alitedesigns.com
Open Friday–Sunday

I find car camping is a great excuse to have a well-stocked slumber party outdoors with friends, and at the end of the night get real sleep on a cushy air mattress in a huge tent – something you can never get away with on a proper backpacking trip. Alite Designs' sleeping bags, tents, chairs and other camp gear are definitely not light. But everything is beautiful and well-made, with just the right mix of nostalgia and modernity. They're still a pretty small company, and so Alite is really into letting people test the gear for free over a weekend. Score.

BAR TARTINE

The new melting pot

561 Valencia Street / (+1) 415 487 1600 / bartartine.com / Open daily

Nick Balla grew up in Michigan and then lived near Budapest for a few years, where his father would make him spicy salads. On his way home from school, the Hungarian street vendors plied him with fried bread topped with sour cream. As an adult, he obsessed over Japanese pub food and became an izakaya chef. Now take all that, stir it in a pot, and what you've got is Bar Tartine. Crazy maybe, but it works. If you've never tried offal, his Japanese-style grilled tripe in a spicy red broth with Hungarian paprika is a better dish than most to deflower your taste buds.

CLAUDIA KUSSANO

Earthy rock candy

591 Guerrero Street / (+1) 415 671 0769 / claudiakussano.com
Closed Monday and Tuesday

Designer Claudia Kussano's jewelry gallery is about as big as a closet-sized bedroom I once rented when I was a student. But as small as it is, I could spend a solid hour here playing dress-up with her earthy and edgy translucent crystals that are wrapped in claw-like hammered bands, not to mention the polished studs and delicate silver leaves, layered to dangle as earrings. Keeping with the nature theme, Claudia tastefully encases her displays in flotsam from the beach or with sweet ferns and petals. My own attempts at bringing the outside in sadly never work quite as well.

DIJITAL FIX

Stereo design and electronics

820 Valencia Street / (+1) 415 666 2256 / dijitalfix.com / Open daily

Walk to the back of this stereo shop, filled with refurbished turntables, speakers, design-forward headphones and amps built into vintage suitcases, and you'll find Tycho, one of the country's most accomplished ambient musicians and an equally talented photographer/designer, in his poster workshop. I've long been a fan of his lithographs and thermal prints of dreamy images inspired by 1970s album artwork, and these are on display at Dijital Fix. Beyond Tycho's prints, the store is really a music lover's playground, with the opportunity to design your own speaker suitcase that they'll then build just for your listening pleasure.

FINE ARTS OPTICAL

Unique eyewear and artist gallery

888 Valencia Street / (+1) 415 913 7414 / fineartsoptical.com
Open daily

My biggest complaint about those preppy Buddy Holly frames everyone seems to be wearing? Everyone seems to be wearing them. Fine Arts Optical has more than 3,000 vintage frames from its 80-year-old Oakland parent company's archives, and is my go-to when I need new glasses. Once I've chosen my new frames I like to check out the reclaimed wood furniture and installations by the other artists with whom Fine Arts shares their soaring gallery space. I could spend hours in the Eames chairs, trying on bejeweled cat eyes from the '50s (show me someone who can pull these off) or the collection of bright plastic rims from the '80s.

MISSION BOWLING CLUB

Rock 'n' roll bar and bowling alley

3176 17th Street / (+1) 415 863 2695 / missionbowlingclub.com
Open daily

From the living wall and sunny patio outside, it's clear before you enter Mission Bowling Club that this is not your average alley. Inside, a gorgeous wooden bar topped with white marble replaces your usual shoe rental station. There are six lanes in the middle of this popular bar but no one's too worried about strikes and funky team shirts. Nah, this is the kind of place where you can bowl to classic rock with plenty of Radiohead in the rotation. Plus the shoes aren't a total embarrassment. You can even knock back a White Russian or munch on a very fancy burger. Now that's my kind of bowling alley.

MR. POLLO

Street food on a tasting menu

2823 Mission Street / (+1) 860 912 9168 / Closed Sunday

There are a lot of fancy four-course tasting menus in this town, but this is by far my favorite. And probably the cheapest at around $15 on average. The combined open kitchen and dining area holds about a dozen people, plus the chef and waiter. Pots and pans are stacked ceiling-high on every shelf. In other words, it's tiny and a little gritty but I swear, each meal is perfection and usually consists of a cold, milled vegetable soup, Little Gems salad and Colombian street foods like crispy arepas. Oh, and the lone waiter doubles up as the pastry chef. How sweet is that?

SALUMERIA

A meat maverick's sandwich counter

3000 20th Street / **(+1) 415 471 2998** / **salumeriasf.com** / **Open daily**

Chef Thomas McNaughton is a hyper-local dreamer. Not only does he cure, cook and bake all of the ingredients for his fancy sandwiches and salads in house, he's also aiming to raise goats on the roof someday. No joke. Personally, I could do without barnyard aromas while I sip wine and dive into a sandwich on the covered patio. As sunny as the Mission is, outdoor seating is rare, so take note. The floor has radiant heating, and the tunes are all classic rock, so even if it isn't a warm summer afternoon, I know I can hang out with a glass of Sancerre and pretend like it is, goat farm or no.

THE NWBLK

The art of retail

1999 Bryant Street / (+1) 415 621 2344 / thenwblk.com
Closed Sunday and Monday

From the outside, this obscure building blends in with many of the other warehouses in this part of the Mission. Inside, The NWBLK can be just as vague. Is it a store? A gallery? A production space? In fact, it's all three. Local and international artists showcase their work, exclusive to The NWBLK, sometimes with production taking place in house. The marriage of make and sell under one roof is especially cool when the manufacturing process is on display next to the finished product. The leather moto jacket was one of the first products for sale in this aesthetically nondescript yet fashion-filled gallery.

THE VOYAGER SHOP

A hybrid of housewares, fashion and rare periodicals

365 Valencia Street / (+1) 415 578 3363 / thevoyagershop.com
Open daily

Revolver, Spartan and Press Works on Paper, all of them independent
retailers, share this space in a kind of permanent pop-up where
no one has to compete for attention or real estate. Often, the cash
register is helmed by one of the owners' friends, and the staff call
The Voyager Shop their island. And the reclaimed wooden dome
that houses magazines and small-batch quarterlies in the back?
Their submarine. Maybe it's magical thinking, but I feel like a kid in
an attic or hideout as I flip through a fantastic collection of indie
publications. Definitely not something you'd see at your regular mall.

WISE SONS

A temple of pastrami and rye

3150 24th Street / (+1) 415 787 3354 / wisesonsdeli.com
Closed Monday and Tuesday

It was love at first slurp when I had my first bowl of matzoh ball soup
in a little Jewish diner outside Chicago and I thought I'd never feel the
same way about another bowl again. That is until two nice boys from
UC Berkeley's Hillel House turned their pastrami pop-up into an official
brick-and-mortar delicatessen in 2013. Wise Sons has a lot of heart,
down to the family portraits hanging on the wall and the hugs given
on your way out. I'm no zaftig, but I don't skimp when I come here for
breakfast or lunch. The decadent chocolate babka and bialys? The bomb.
And the matzoh? Divine.

Aa

is for

ppenzeller

Bb

is for

brie

Ch

is

che

CUESA
1 Ferry Building, (+1) 415 291 3276, cuesa.org, Saturday classes

FIRST CLASS COOKING
1 Bluxome Street, (+1) 415 573 2453, emilydellas.com,
check website for class schedule

FLOUR + WATER
2401 Harrison Street, (+1) 415 826 7000, flourandwater.com,
check website for class schedule

THE CHEESE SCHOOL OF SAN FRANCISCO
2124 Folsom Street, (+1) 415 346 7530, cheeseschoolsf.com,
check website for class schedule

cooking classes

Learn new kitchen skills from the city's favorite chefs

If you travel to San Francisco to eat, consider staying to cook too. Thanks to its awesome produce, the Bay Area attracts people who want to understand and appreciate food on a deeper level, professionally or just for pleasure. Simply sit down with a menu at any restaurant outside of the tourist traps, and the servers (sometimes even the bus boys) will wax on about how the cows who made the organic milk in your cheese spend their days grazing on the coastal cliffs of Point Reyes. Not to mention how the sous chef selected the milk personally and then let it soft ripen into a triple cream laced with mushrooms she foraged herself. It's a lot to take in before you've even ordered. But one of the benefits of being in a city filled with chefs and restaurants that fetishize all things local and artisanal is that chances are, on any given day, someone's teaching a class. For example, Thomas McNaughton of Salumeria (see page 48) leads a pasta-making class and intimate dinner in the "dough room" of his nearby restaurant **Flour + Water** (a good option if you can't get a hard-to-come-by table reservation there). Others, such as **First Class Cooking**, invite drop-in students into the chef's home kitchen to prepare, say, a Provençal dinner complete with French onion soup, coq au vin and chocolate soufflé. On most Saturdays, the **Center for Urban Education about Sustainable Agriculture (CUESA)** holds free open-air classes, taught by an area restaurant chef at the Ferry Building farmers market. And if you're going to be in town for a few days, consider taking a weekend workshop on types of cheese or cheese-making at **The Cheese School of San Francisco** – wine pairings included!

castro

noe valley, bernal heights, glen park

These areas make up what I call "the cute" districts. The ones you'd live in if you dream of settling down near a main street with equal parts yoga studios, organic produce markets, bookstores and parks. Glen Park wins for best grocery store and running trails, while Bernal Heights gets best bakery and dog park. Noe Valley, with its quaint shopping village and cozy neighborhood restaurants, is perhaps the most charming, but its neighbor, the Castro proper takes the cake for the best party scene in the city. The Castro is also a great place to start if you're looking to explore the LBGTQ scene and some of SF's most impeccably kept Victorian mansions.

1 Canyon Market
2 Contigo
3 Fiat Lux
4 Frances
5 Isso
6 MAAS & Stacks
7 Omnivore Books on Food
8 Sandbox Bakery
9 Sui Generis Consignment
10 Unionmade

55

CANYON MARKET

Niche deli and grocer

2815 Diamond Street / (+1) 415 586 9999 / canyonmarket.com
Open daily

A few years ago I interviewed food scientist extraordinaire Harold McGee (the man behind *On Food and Cooking* and *The New York Times'* Curious Cook column) at his house in San Francisco. He made me a simple salad of gorgeous greens dressed in garlic and a bright olive oil he found at a neighborhood market that's little-known south of the Mission. Canyon Market comes from ex-restaurant industry folks and attracts pros as well as serious home cooks with their hard-to-find stock of wines and pantry staples. Serious eaters, like me, head straight to the huge deli case and sandwich counter.

CONTIGO

Tapas in a romantic setting

1320 Castro Street / (+1) 415 285 0250 / contigosf.com
Closed Monday

As a restaurant reviewer, it's hard for people to find new places to take me for an evening. My now boyfriend told me so the first time we went for dinner, but he scored 10 points off the bat for introducing me to Contigo. The Spanish tapas are your usual suspects, but it's the green, dimly lit covered patio where we ate that made that first date so memorable. That and the Tempranillo-swigging waiter who humored us as we tried to pinpoint his accent. A year later, my boyfriend and I returned. To the same table and the same waiter, who very sweetly pretended to remember us.

FIAT LUX

Wrought rings with an edge

218 Church Street / (+1) 415 312 8413 / fiatluxsf.com / Closed Tuesday

When Alexei Angelides tries to define his store, he scrunches up his nose: "It's like Etsy but not as precious." I know what he means. In the past few years, there's a definite style that's emerged from the online craft emporium. As a result, a lot of prints and jewelry have started to look alike: i.e. a little cutesy and homespun. The goods in Fiat Lux on the other hand are edgy, elegant and exquisitely crafted. Instead of platinum, they use brass. Instead of 5-karat diamond engagement rings, there are love knot rings, a design from the 1920s. I have a feeling it won't be long before imitations pop up on Etsy.

FRANCES

Late-night supper club

3870 17th Street / (+1) 415 621 3870 / frances-sf.com
Closed Monday

If I had to eat at just one restaurant every night, hands down it would be Frances. First of all, it's on a darling tree-lined street in the Castro. Second, this is food and wine worth luxuriating over. But the reality is, I had to wait a month just to get a 10:30 dinner reservation for four. I arrived slightly weary, and upon seeing me, the most professional, warm waiter I've ever met handed me chickpea frites and a glass of cava. Seated and relaxed, we ordered one of everything and without feeling rushed, we talked, we drank and we ate, and finally left at 1:30am.

ISSO

SF-made and vintage wardrobe

3789 24th Street / (+1) 415 920 9149 / issosf.com / Open daily

Lately, I've been obsessed with Ossie Clark dresses and long-sleeved minis from the 1970s. The girls at Isso have promised to be on the lookout for me when they do their scouting for clothes from the '60s through '90s. They get new stuff in every day, and they have a tendency of pulling dresses and skirts for you to try, for no other reason than to see what their vintage treasures look like on. The other day, they draped me in a sleeveless summer dress, matched it with a cool leather belt, and added a punchy leather clutch. It was kind of like a roommate letting you raid her very well-stocked closet, only better.

MAAS & STACKS

Curated everyday style

2128 Market Street / (+1) 415 678 5629 / maasandstacks.com
Closed Monday

The Castro has no shortage of stylish men. Two of them are Otto Gustav Zoell and Stephen Chen. The jetsetters were in Japan years ago when they discovered designers and clothing makers they'd never heard of before in the States. When they got back to San Francisco, they brought the Japanese labels with them and opened MAAS & Stacks, a white, streamlined men's boutique at the gateway of the Castro. For all its pristine-ness, the store's staff doesn't take itself too seriously. These are tailored, well-crafted clothes and denim in cool cuts for a kind of casual luxury Kanye West might embrace.

OMNIVORE BOOKS ON FOOD

A gourmand's cookbook heaven

**3885a Cesar Chavez Street / (+1) 415 282 4712 / omnivorebooks.com
Open daily**

Some people collect vintage heels and dresses. For others, it's vinyl. Me?
Rare, old cookbooks. Much of what lines my long block counter at home
comes from Celia Sack's butcher-turned-bookshop, Omnivore Books on
Food. My prized title is a 1960s illustrated children's cookbook that's half in
French, half English. Celia also helped me snag highly coveted first editions
of Jacques Pepin's *La Technique* and *A Gentleman's Companion*, two heady
volumes of early 20th-century cocktails and cookery. She's got my email
and lets me know when she's got something good in. But sometimes,
I don't wait for an email and just wander over to browse.

SANDBOX BAKERY

Pastries, Japanese style

**833 Cortland Avenue / (+1) 415 642 8580 / sandboxbakerysf.com
Open daily**

The vibe in Bernal Heights is a little earthy and crunchy. Read: a lot of stretchy yoga pants and organic baby slings. So I was surprised to come across a corner beacon of Japanese modernity in Sandbox Bakery. It's a beautiful space that makes you want to linger, though only a few people can fit inside. In the pastry display case are some classic goodies, such as scones and muffins, and Japanese-inspired treats, with curry, sage, yuzu or miso. If you get there before all the yoga moms snap them up, order a rice burger. It's a sandwich with rice patties for bread, perfect for the neighborhood's gluten-free crowd.

SUI GENERIS CONSIGNMENT

High fashion on a budget

2231 and 2265 Market Street / (+1) 415 437 2231
suigenerisconsignment.com / Open daily

I love a good treasure hunt, especially when it comes to second-hand stores. Shopping at Sui Generis' pair of consignment shops for men and women is like entering some fabulous museum closet. Previously worn pieces are displayed like art, and there are some new pieces from local Academy of Art alums. Toward the back of both stores (just a few doors away from each other) are your more everyday labels like J. Crew and Calvin Klein. I've heard stories of men finding Gucci suits and friends spotting designer boots for less than the cost of a weekly shop at Whole Foods.

UNIONMADE

All-American good looks

493 Sanchez Street / (+1) 415 861 3373 / unionmadegoods.com
Open daily

Since it opened, Unionmade has been something of a boys club.
And if this clubhouse had a uniform, it would include cuffed denim,
an urban cowboy collared shirt and handcrafted leather accessories
like the ones your father, grandfather and great grandfather had. Then
Unionmade expanded its membership with tailored shirts and bags
from their little offshoot called The Mill up the hill in Noe Valley. For
now, my unisex Chester Wallace bag (designed to fit a six-pack, no less)
accompanies me practically everywhere I go.

lgbtq in sf

Everyday pride

During the last week of every June, the Pride celebration takes over San Francisco, most notably with a fabulous parade that rolls down Market Street from Beale to 8th Streets. Starting at 10:30am on a Saturday, the party keeps going through to early Tuesday morning. But even if you're not in town for the extravaganza, you can get a taste of Pride any night of the week at dance clubs like **San Francisco Badlands** and **The Lookout** (both in the Castro), or lesbian dive bar **The Lexington Club** (in the Mission). San Francisco Badlands is in the heart of the Castro, often thought of as LGBTQ HQ. The homes in the neighborhood itself look prim and proper, but inside the club it's all strobe lights and shirtless men fueled by strong drinks from the bar. The Lookout is small and more laid back, a great spot for dancing on a weeknight and a smidge removed from the center of the scene.

On the weekends, check out the Speedo sunbathers on the upper terrace at **Dolores Park**, affectionately known as The Fruit Shelf. Be sure to visit the Spanish colonial baroque stylings of **The Castro Theatre**, which hosts LGBTQ community events and movie sing-alongs most nights.

Beyond these hubs, you don't have to look very hard to experience San Francisco's "love one, love all" attitude. Yes, the Castro is the historic center, but the community spreads far beyond – unlike many other cities that can still feel somewhat segregated. Here in San Francisco, it's well represented in all corners, from City Hall, where same-sex marriage ceremonies take place, to Dogpatch, Sunset and Haight.

DOLORES PARK
Between 18th and 20th Streets, and Dolores and Church Streets, sfrecpark.org/destination/mission-dolores-park

SAN FRANCISCO BADLANDS
4121 18th Street, (+1) 415 626 9320, sfbadlands.com, open daily

THE CASTRO THEATRE
429 Castro Street, (+1) 415 621 6120, castrotheatre.com, open daily

THE LEXINGTON CLUB
3464 19th Street, (+1) 415 863 2052, lexingtonclub.com, open daily

THE LOOKOUT
3600 16th Street, (+1) 415 431 0306, thelookoutsf.com, open daily

CASTRO

haight

hayes valley, cole valley, haight-ashbury, nopa

The four hoods that make up the larger Haight are very different from each other. Hayes Valley has a quiet refinement and plenty of shopping, while North of Panhandle (NoPa) remains brash and artsy – a place where you can grab a $20 burger, see Macklemore perform live and stock up your wardrobe with head-to-toe local designs. Last but not least, compared to the raucous (famously so, since the summer of love) Haight-Ashbury, Cole Valley is more like a quaint village, and is full of great places to eat.

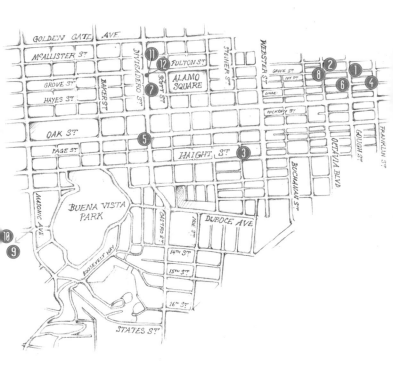

1 Boxing Room
2 Kappa Zakka
3 Maven
4 Nojo
5 Ragazza
6 Rand + Statler

7 Rare Device
8 Reliquary
9 Tantrum (off map)
10 The Ice Cream Bar (off map)
11 The Mill
12 The Perish Trust

BOXING ROOM

A taste of the bayou

399 Grove Street / (+1) 415 430 6590 / boxingroom.com / Open daily

I'm all for local, organic, humanely raised ingredients that have been sung to and massaged before they end up on the plate. I get it. I really do. But sometimes, no offense eco-licious stalwarts, it's all so precious that I just want to sit down to an awesome meal and not have to listen to some waiter rattle off what a great life my food had. Cue Boxing Room, a huge restaurant (by SF standards anyway) that serves fatty duck jambalayas and other Louisiana-inspired dishes (a lot of it fried or raw seafood) that'll stick to your ribs. Think of it as refined but casual Creole cuisine made by a native Southerner who's somehow made alligator taste so fresh and delicious, you'd guess it was local.

KAPPA ZAKKA

Handicraft kitsch and things

460 Grove Street / **(+1) 415 735 5795** / **Closed Monday and Tuesday**

One of the best parts of this job is that I get to wander and rediscover neighborhoods I haven't been to in a while. Hayes Valley is one of those areas of continual discovery, where I can find myself taking a road I'm not sure I've ever been down and stumble upon a hidden gem. One day during our research for this book, Meghan and I had stopped to consult our map when we looked up and saw Kappa Zakka, a long and narrow curiosity shop with a minimalist bent. I love the mix of Nordic and Japanese wares, some practical and some just beautiful tchotchkes for the home. A great discovery that I intend to find my way back to, often.

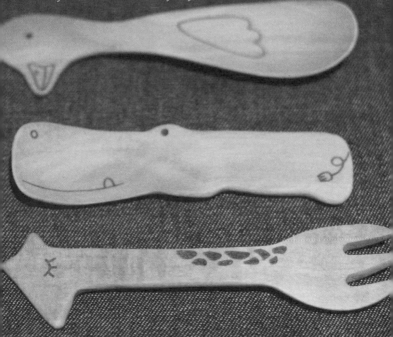

MAVEN

Eats to go with your drinks

598 Haight Street / (+1) 415 829 7982 / maven-sf.com / Open daily

The long communal tables at Maven are consistently jam-packed. I'd been up and down Haight Street and dying for something other than barbecue and coffee shop sandwiches when I saw an empty seat by the window. I snagged it and dove into the menu. It's split into three columns, with food down the middle, a cocktail pairing on the left and a wine or beer pairing on the right. Genius if you ask me. The food is New American small plates with a few surprises, such as Chinatown duck sliders, but Maven is more of a bar that serves food than the other way round. The hip, sceney vibe makes it ideal for first dates or a place to warm up for the night before hitting the neighborhood's dive bars.

∩OJO

Farm-fresh yakitori house

231 Franklin Street / (+1) 415 896 4587 / nojosf.com / Closed Tuesday

I love a good sushi or ramen joint, but Japanese pubs (called izayakas) are where I want to be at the end of a long day. Nojo is just the ticket, thanks to their cold beer, sake and crispy chicken. For Nojo, which means "farm" in Japanese, chef-owner Greg Dunmore does some kushiyaki (literally, "grilled on a stick") with simple, basic spices and kicks it way up on others with big, bold flavors. As the name implies, the produce is locally sourced and farm-fresh, which gives this Japanese menu a decidedly elevated Californian twist. So is it traditional? The food not so much, but the lively scene is definitely authentic.

RAGAZZA

Pizza al fresco

311 Divisadero Street / (+1) 415 255 1133 / ragazzasf.com / Open daily

Every neighborhood needs a good pizza place. I'm not talking about a rundown spot that serves soggy crusts with oily cheese and pepperoni. No, my version of Friday pizza night is slightly more gourmet. Ragazza means "girl" in Italian, and on the wall are black-and-white pictures of the owner as one, along with others of her mamma and family. It's hard to get a seat inside to check them out though (this place seems to open its doors already packed). Luckily, in the back is that rarest of rare SF treasures: an open patio. I'm happy to luxuriate there any night of the week.

RAND + STATLER

A little bit of SoHo in SF

425 Hayes Street / (+1) 415 634 0881 / randandstatler.com
Open daily

Compared to New Yorkers, most San Franciscans are no fashionistas. Blame the fog or the proximity to Lake Tahoe, but we like our shoes flat, North Face fleeces warm and bags hand-stitched. Better yet if what we wear is organic or made of upcycled materials. When we do get dressed up, though, we like to keep it simple and chic. Rand + Statler hosts elegant, on-trend looks, including refined but edgy black Rick Owens cutaway gowns. The store is a spacious and upscale emporium of the sartorial arts — just check out their impressive collection of fashion coffee-table books. The shoes: a mix of fanciful heels and yes, flats.

RARE DEVICE

Small-batch artist collaborative

600 Divisadero Street / (+1) 415 863 3969 / raredevice.net
Open daily

When Rare Device moved into the NoPa area, a new moniker came into play: the Design Corridor. Looking around the neighborhood, you'll see a lot of shops that focus on local designers and objects of desire, but Rare Device is the anchor amidst all the whimsy. A gallery wall at the back features a different artist's work each month, and you can always count on Rare Device to have an interesting pop-up shop inside, giving you a new reason to revisit often.

RELIQUARY

Bohemian-chic boutique

537 Octavia Street / **(+1) 415 431 4000** / **reliquarysf.com** / **Open daily**

This is everything a women's boutique should be: a mix of new
bohemian and vintage in a comfortably sized space. Reliquary owner
Leah Bershad handpicks everything, including out-of-this-world Moroccan
rugs. They're made of old house carpets, mashed up by artisans into
colorful and funky new ones — some of them with glitter and dust still
in them. But, really, this is a house of fashion that's full of Southwestern
prints, incense and pretty jewelry with 1970s biker rock glamor. And a
sacred house at that, as the name Reliquary suggests.

TANTRUM

Cool kids' toy box

858 Cole Street / (+1) 415 504 6980 / shoptantrum.com / Open daily

One of the best parts of being friends with someone who has kids is having an excuse to buy toys. There's a lot of new stuff out there, but I get a thrill every time I come across old analog toys that I remember playing with as a child and seeing that they're still in production. Usually they're replicas or reissues of things like a Playskool turntable or camera. Tantrum carries those, but they also seek out the originals to sell in their minimalist toyshop. Original or not, my friends' kids totally dig the sherbet-colored records that come with the Playskool players I buy for them from here.

THE ICE CREAM BAR

Homemade frozen treats and sodas

815 Cole Street   (+1) 415 742 4932   theicecreambarsf.com
Open daily

This city has no shortage of artisan creameries, most of them scooping flavors for shock value (Boccalone prosciutto, anyone?). But sometimes, all I want is a classic sundae, one without controversy or bits of cured meat. Pastry chef Juliet Pries' 1930s-inspired The Ice Cream Bar is all about a time when chocolate tasted like chocolate and soda fountains looked more like bars. Hey, people had to go somewhere during Prohibition. OK, so everything's organic and made in small batches. Yes, there are rows of botanical extracts that the soda jerks mix into tonics. But the splits and tall floats are sweet enough to bring back memories of simpler times.

THE MILL

Fancy toast club

736 Divisadero Street / (+1) 415 345 1953 / themillsf.com / Open daily

I know what you're thinking: toast is toast. But Josey Baker makes art of it. The Mill is his ode to slices fresh from the oven. Like a bagel house, there are toppings to choose from. Combos include butter and sea salt on aromatic cinnamon raisin bread or almond butter on wholewheat. But my favorite is a super dark rye with fluffy cream cheese. The Mill is also the best place to grab a fruity, light Four Barrel roast. Which is probably why this place seems to attract a lot of artist and writer types, known for living off coffee and buttered bread alone.

THE PERISH TRUST

Whimsical treasures

728 Divisadero Street / (+1) 415 400 5225 / theperishtrust.com
Closed Monday

I'm a huge fan of all things old and well-worn. Maybe it's because I've
inherited so many family antiques. I remember spending afternoons
wandering my grandparents' dark and drafty house – their frugality with
electricity a holdover from the Great Depression – and playing with their
old artifacts, among them a spinning wheel from the turn of the century.
I get the same sense of mystery and discovery at The Perish Trust in this up-
and-coming stretch of Divisadero. In an alcove is a Warby Parker spectacle
showroom, one of just a few in the nation. If you're all set on glasses, you'll
still enjoy the rare periodicals and mid-priced trinkets.

san francisco after dark

The best of the city's cocktail culture

No one has a better happy hour than **Biergarten** in Hayes Valley, where the picnic tables are always full and the makeshift kitchen (in an old shipping container!) churns out baskets of hot pretzels and brats. Just after sunset, the white lights strung across the patio come on, and the temperature drops quickly. There are no heat lamps here, so one of the nice bartenders will bring around heavy blankets to keep everyone warm. It's all very Kumbaya minus the bonfire, but with excellent beers served in large steins (some of them bigger than your head).

If I'm going to a concert at The Fillmore, I like to pregame at **Fat Angel**, a low-key gastro pub with 150 brews and old church pews for seating. In fact, the whole place is outfitted with salvaged furniture – and organ pipes – from a 1910 church that was demolished for condos outside Napa. A nighttime café, Fat Angel is the kind of place you go to actually talk, preferably over a cracker-thin flatbread that's topped with roasted grapes, prosciutto, walnuts and gorgonzola perfect for sharing.

Fat Angel

BIERGARTEN
424 Octavia Street, (+1) 415 252 9289, biergartensf.com,
closed Monday and Tuesday

DNA LOUNGE
375 11th Street, (+1) 415 626 1409, dnalounge.com,
check the online calendar

FAT ANGEL
1740 O'Farrell Street, (+1) 415 525 3013, fatangelsf.com,
open daily

RICKSHAW STOP
155 Fell Street, (+1) 415 861 2011, rickshawstop.com,
check the online calendar

THE CHAPEL
777 Valencia Street, (+1) 415 551 5157, thechapelsf.com,
open daily

TRICK DOG
3010 20th Street, (+1) 415 471 2999, trickdogbar.com,
open daily

For dancing, I'm a fan of **DNA Lounge** late at night in SoMa or **Rickshaw Stop** in Hayes Valley, where you're as likely to catch Grizzly Bear playing a random show as you are to walk into an Indian techno dance night. Either way, you're drinking cheap beer or vodka tonics.

But my new favorite venue is on Valencia Street at **The Chapel**, a combination of beer garden, sit-down New American restaurant and concert hall. Afterward, it's a 10-minute walk to **Trick Dog**, where the artisanal cocktail menu is designed like a record album and the drinks are inspired by culinary flavor combos, such as tequila, bay leaf and lime.

pacific heights

western addition, japantown, fillmore, cow hollow, marina

The Pac Heights crowd skews a little more traditional than the rest of the city and prides itself on its Victorian mansions and beautiful view of the Marina. The college crowd dominates the Marina and Cow Hollow, but there are plenty of grown-up shops around to balance it out. For culture, your best bets are the Fillmore, with its jazz roots, and Japantown, where you can do everything from taking a soak at a Japanese bath house to exploring J-pop culture.

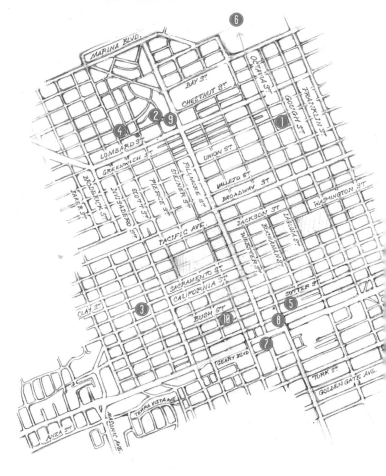

1   Freda Salvador
2   Le Marais Bakery
3   March
4   Marine Layer
5   New People

6   Off the Grid (off map)
7   State Bird Provisions
8   Suzu
9   Tacolicious
10 Timeless Treasures

FREDA SALVADOR

European leather boots

1782 Union Street / (+1) 415 654 5128 / fredasalvador.com
Closed Sunday

The low boot is the perfect year-round shoe in the Bay Area, and the two-woman team behind Freda Salvador makes the best. Every year, Megan and Cristina attend Lineapelle in Bologna, Italy, to find the best calf hairs and exotic leathers to build their gorgeous boots (and some oxfords and loafers). They then take their designs and materials to Elda, Spain, where their four collections are produced. On a recent visit, the ladies showed me designs for their upcoming resort collection. The sneak peek did not disappoint, revealing what might be the next quintessential San Francisco shoe: leather high tops, perfect for climbing the city's pavement hills.

LE MARAIS BAKERY

Parisian boulangerie by the bay

2066 Chestnut Street / (+1) 415 359 9801 / lemaraisbakery.com
Open daily

Even in Paris, it can be something of a hunt to find a decent croque monsieur, that lovely stack of brioche, ham, béchamel and melted cheese that's made to be eaten at a sidewalk café with an espresso on the side. More often than not, what you get is a dry cheese sandwich with a meager dollop of sauce. But Le Marais Bakery, named after the bohemian Parisian neighborhood, turns out a pretty spectacular version. Theirs comes on a thick slice of pain de mie, smeared with wholegrain mustard, covered with house-sliced ham, a thin béchamel and a generous sprinkling of gruyère – grilled first, then finished off in the oven. C'est magnifique.

MARCH

Exquisite housewares

3075 Sacramento Street / (+1) 415 931 7433 / marchsf.com
Closed Sunday

The queen of the Bay Area's slow food movement scene is Alice Waters, the lady behind Chez Pannise. Since the '70s, she's championed simple, organic, and seasonal food, inspiring young chefs including Sam Hamilton, the man behind March who once interned at Waters' iconic Berkeley restaurant. At March, Sam has created an artisan cookery and dining store with a working Aga stove that makes it feel like an open kitchen – one with a pantry of own-label olive oils and preserves. All the modern wares and cooking tools on the shelves look and feel special to the touch, and are made to last for generations.

MARINE LAYER

Perfect-fitting basics

2209 Chestnut Street / (+1) 415 346 2400 / marinelayer.com
Open daily

I admire urban legends that start with a fledgling pop-up business and end with a gorgeous storefront and a faithful following. And so it goes for Marine Layer and its super soft threads. Mike Natenshon started hawking his cozy shirts and beach sweaters out of his apartment in 2009 and then took them online, where the orders started piling up. The style is definitely casual and laid back, just like the city itself. (For example, someone once suggested I use a Marine Layer's infinity scarf as a yoga loop.) I like to go here to shop for basics and something to cuddle up in at the next bonfire at nearby Baker Beach.

NEW PEOPLE THE STORE

J-pop culture bonanza

**1746 Post Street / (+1) 415 525 8630 / newpeopleworld.com
Open daily**

Most people don't make it past the noodle joints in the Japantown mall, much less the furniture stores and galleries, to see that the real J-pop crowd is hanging out across the street at the white monolith that is the New People building. The five shops inside (there's also a small cinema and café) run the gamut from Japanese Lolita to anime goth. The largest is New People The Store on the first floor. It's chock full of elegantly designed cookwares, lots of collector's toys and a huge selection of sleek home accessories that I've seen only in shops a tenth this size. All of it imported from Japan, naturally.

OFF THE GRID

Weekly street-food party

Fort Mason Center / (+1) 415 339 5888 / offthegridsf.com
Open Friday 5pm–10pm (closed for winter)

Matt Cohen's love for street food started in Japan, where he became obsessed with ramen served out of cars fitted with fire pits. When he moved back to the U.S., the mobile food craze was picking up speed, and the city was scattered with trucks and carts selling everything from Asian hot wings to delicate crème brûlée. So in 2010, Matt brought the trucks together to launch Off the Grid. Every Friday, more than 30 food sellers and a pop-up beer garden set up in Fort Mason's parking lot, attracting a mix of hipsters, families and frat types. Hint: bring napkins, and wear an old shirt. Eating sans dining table can get messy.

STATE BIRD PROVISIONS

A movable feast with California pride

1529 Fillmore Street / (+1) 415 795 1272 / statebirdsf.com / Open daily

I like to spend late Sunday morning reading the paper and eating dim sum. I can sit for hours with the Style sections while a whimsical dance of carts, each offering different dishes, takes place around me. The same dance happens at James Beard Award winner State Bird Provisions. Except for a few shared plates on a menu of commandables, service is by cart and tray, like a dim sum house, except here dim sum itself is not served. It's fun to anticipate what's coming next, as the food is global in flavor, although California's state bird, the quail, makes it onto the menu. Unsurprising really, given the joint's name. Fresh fish and seafood is presented outside the box thanks to Asian preparations, such as a spicy Dungeness crab kimchi with bright notes of yuba and smoked egg.

SUZU

For the noodle-obsssessed

1581 Webster Street / (+1) 415 346 5083 / Closed Tuesday

As a writer, I get to interview a lot of people with cool jobs. Lately, it's been the trending executive chefs from some of San Francisco's most popular kitchens, and I've been quizzing them about where they eat when they're not working. Suzu, a glassed-in noodle house at the west entrance of the Japantown mall, is the name I'm hearing most often. After cooking all day, it seems what chefs want is something simple and classic. That is, shoyu ramen with egg and scallions. What makes it a chef fave is the perfect pork and soy sauce-based broth. And the house-made noodles? Thin and just a little springy. Yum.

TACOLICIOUS

Mexi-Cali tacos and tequila bar

2031 Chestnut Street / (+1) 415 346 1966 / tacolicious.com
Open daily

When I'm in Mexico, my favorite late-night meal is street-side tacos, perfect for soaking up the tequila. Two soft corn tortillas topped with juicy, braised chicken or beef, cabbage and salsa? Nothing could be simpler or fresher. Despite the name, and the absence of burritos, Tacolicious is no taqueria. Think of it as Mexico City style tacos with a gringo twist. By the copper-topped bar, there's usually a professional baseball player or two getting down to a plate of soft tacos and a beer. That brings in the sports fans that are starting or (more often than not) ending a night out.

TIMELESS TREASURES

Antiques from Paris and beyond

**2176 Sutter Street / (+1) 415 775 8366 / timelesstreasuressf.com
Open daily**

I've hunted for a lot of things in my life: the perfect partner, apartments and even pheasants, believe it or not. You could say that Joan O'Connor is a hunter, too. She scours the world over for antiques and little items that she must have looked into every nook and cranny to unearth. It's fun to meander through Timeless Treasures, her long sliver of a shop, and search ceiling to floor for the perfect something. She gets in fresh stuff, mostly antiques but some modern things as well, every day — from the Bay Area, Boston and France — so there's always something new to discover.

urban hikes

Take in the view at the top of SF's best hills

BERNAL HEIGHTS PARK (BERNAL HEIGHTS)
COIT TOWER (NORTH BEACH)
GLEN CANYON (GLEN PARK)
LANDS END (RICHMOND)
TWIN PEAKS (CASTRO)

Whenever I've been guilty of overeating or in desperate need of some hard exercise, I climb the 475 feet up the winding path to the top of **Bernal Heights Park**, a hill that remains green through winter and turns gold come summer. On the north side, you get a sweeping view of the city, all the way from the Golden Gate to the Bay Bridge. To the west, you'll see another famous hill worth climbing: **Twin Peaks**. (If it's not blanketed by fog, it's the one with the big red radio tower.) Of the two, I prefer Bernal. Here, dogs happily wander off-leash, and couples cuddle in the tall grass. I always feel refreshed when I walk down to the bottom again, almost as if I've just been for a hike in Muir Woods. In reality the park is just a few blocks from the 24th Street BART station. Some of my other favorite climbs include the groomed trails inside **Glen Canyon**. Park your car near the Safeway supermart, and take any pathway uphill. Or if you're feeling really athletic, work up to the cracks and routes where actual climbers spider monkey their way to the top, sans rope. For something less challenging and just as scenic, I like to mosey along the forested **Lands End** trails near the water in the northwest corner of the city. Of course, because San Francisco is dotted with hills and is a city, there are plenty of concrete hikes with nary a tree in sight. The best is the ascent to **Coit Tower** in North Beach, where you get the added bonus of taking in Diego Rivera murals along with a bay view at the peak.

the avenues

sunset, richmond, presidio

Golden Gate Park begins at Stanyan Street, denoting (more or less) the beginning of the outlier residential areas known as The Avenues. To the south of the park is the Sunset, a foggy enclave dotted with ranch houses that run all the way to Ocean Beach, where a group of surfer-craftspeople have made a home. North of the park is the Richmond, where you'll find the best dim sum and noodles outside of Chinatown. The Presidio, which sits at the northeast corner of the Richmond, is the quietest of the lot. It's an old army base surrounded by redwoods and eucalyptus trees; a forest in the middle of the city.

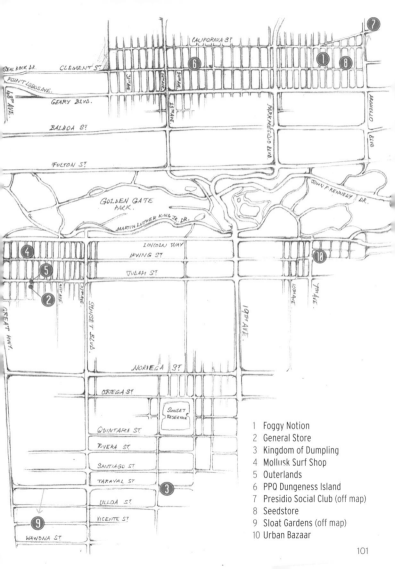

1 Foggy Notion
2 General Store
3 Kingdom of Dumpling
4 Mollusk Surf Shop
5 Outerlands
6 PPQ Dungeness Island
7 Presidio Social Club (off map)
8 Seedstore
9 Sloat Gardens (off map)
10 Urban Bazaar

FOGGY NOTION

Handmade everything

275 6th Avenue / (+1) 415 683 5654 / Closed Monday and Tuesday

At Foggy Notion, there are several rows of Mason jars in all their forms, including (get this) a hand-soap dispenser. They really are lovely, especially standing next to the other handmade, eco-friendly treasures inside. Almost everything is local and made by the owner's friends or herself. See, Alissa Anderson (a popular photographer and stylist) sold so many of her sporty wallets and leather clutches (upcycled from tennis racket bags and rum pouches) to boutiques around the city that she eventually had to open her own shop. Besides her bags, the tiny storefront displays things she truly loves and can't live without. And that apparently includes Mason jars.

GENERAL STORE

Laid-back designs by laid-back designers

**4035 Judah Street / (+1) 415 682 0600 / shop-generalstore.com
Open daily**

Hipsters are to the Mission what surfers and craftsmen are to the Sunset. There must be something about the ocean that attracts artists and woodworkers — all of them dreamy and tan, of course. The thing is, they really are making gorgeous stuff. Most of it's displayed at General Store, a design boutique of some 200, well, "things". Everything here, including the wood tunnel that acts as a walk-through magazine stand, has an artistic touch. So, too, does the backyard's tiny greenhouse — barely big enough for two people to stand in — made of reclaimed doors and windows by an up-and-coming artist. Naturally.

KINGDOM OF DUMPLING

The real deal on dim sum

**1713 Taraval Street / (+1) 415 566 6143 / kingofchinesedumpling.com
Open daily**

Despite the name, this pocket of a restaurant is anything but regal. Queue for one of 20 seats, and then quickly order a dozen or so steamed *xiao long bao* (Shanghai soup dumplings) – while attentive, it can feel like the staff's rushing you to move the line outside. Your table will soon be covered with inelegant plates of steamed white lotus-shaped blobs with no frills or garnish. But trust me – when you take a bite into the thin dumpling wrappers that have just the right amount of chew, be sure to have your soup spoon handy. You don't want to miss a drop of these beauties!

MOLLUSK SURF SHOP

Find your endless summer

4500 Irving Street / (+1) 415 564 6300 / mollusksurfshop.com
Open daily

Last time I tried surfing, it was at surf camp in Australia. I managed to get up on my board easily at first, but after three days, my arms and legs would give out before I could pop up to a stand. It didn't help either that the foam board made contact with my face a few times. So my career hanging 10 was short lived. And yet, I feel more than welcome at Mollusk Surf Shop, where vintage boards as well as more modern ones made by local shapers attract true wave-riders, and kooks like me can marvel at the dry-land fashions and funky indoor treehouse.

OUTERLANDS

Ocean Beach's best warming hut

**4001 Judah Street / (+1) 415 661 6140 / outerlandssf.com
Closed Monday**

In keeping with the Sunset's driftwood theme, walking into Outerlands used to be like entering a lone sea shanty. But with a new parklet and a recent expansion into an old Chinese restaurant next door, that shanty has become a proper beach home. One with a killer weekend brunch, thanks to the house-made pain au levain baked by owner Dave Muller. All the loaves are crusty outside and have an inside that's made for tearing apart. I like to wrap myself in one of the blankets by the door and dip a thick slice of toast in one of the seasonal fish stews for instant warmth.

PPQ DUNGENESS ISLAND

The ultimate Vietnamese crab fest

2332 Clement Street / (+1) 415 386 8266 / ppqcrab.com / Open daily

Food-wise, November is my favorite month. It's the start of crab season, and the place to go is PPQ Dungeness Island. You get to choose what sauce your just-caught crab is cooked in: think roasted garlic, peppercorn or drawn butter. I went with my friend and her Vietnamese cousins, who all insisted on getting big bowls of buttery garlic noodles, as well as fried chicken feet. Two hours later, we had demolished four crabs and several dozen pounds of noodles. On the way out, I looked back at the debris we'd left, but the waiter was already pouring tea on the strewn table and wiping it clean so that everything smelled of bergamot.

PRESIDIO SOCIAL CLUB

Old-fashioned standards made special

**563 Ruger Street / (+1) 415 885 1888 / presidiosocialclub.com
Open daily**

In the 1940s, Building 563 was used as barracks on the Presidio army base. Today, it welcomes those who yearn for the days of big bands and the American bistro fare our grandparents still rave about. Most people opt for a booth, but I love sitting at the long marble bar with an old-fashioned martini (the greatest code word for "straight vodka in a glass") and eating humble dishes, like mashed peas with mint. There are more contemporary offerings too, including a savory *banh mi* (a Vietnamese filled baguette) but it's their high-low take on a Sloppy Joe, quite refined in the throw-back interior, that I can't resist.

SEEDSTORE

Americana rags for men and women

212 Clement Street / (+1) 415 386 1600 / seedstoresf.com
Open daily

I'm an only child, so I never had a big sister whose closet I could raid on a whim. But if I had, I'd have wanted its contents to resemble Seedstore's stocks. Perhaps it's no coincidence that the owners are sisters who share great style. They will happily put together outfits for you that at first seem outrageously mismatched but once on, always work beautifully. As a bonus, the store also has a collection of reclaimed housewares and a rotating art gallery. There's plenty for guys, too — though I've never met a man who coveted his brother's threads enough to "borrow" them behind his back.

SLOAT GARDENS

The wannabe gardener's paradise

**2700 Sloat Boulevard / (+1) 415 566 4415 / sloatgardens.com
Open daily**

I was once known as a plant killer. If it was green and alive when it entered my apartment, it would surely leave brown and dead within weeks. When I moved to a more light-filled house with a backyard, I was determined to turn my reputation around. Green-fingered friends pointed me to Sloat Gardens, an institution in a town obsessed with homesteading and fire escape herb gardens. The people who work here can tell you what to grow in what microclimate, down to the seed varietal and city block. Now, I'm proud to say, my backyard has a bountiful vegetable box and blooming roses year round.

URBAN BAZAAR

Gifts for do-gooders

**1371 9th Avenue / (+1) 415 664 4422 / urbanbazaarsf.com
Open daily**

This city has a reputation for loving all things local, sustainable
and fair trade – whether we're talking slippers, holiday decorations,
greeting cards, jewelry or even sunglasses. Urban Bazaar is clearly a
gift shop with those ideals in mind. The knitted kids' hats made to look
like zoo animals are charming, but what I couldn't resist were the knit
crocodile slippers when I saw that they came in adult sizes as well.
They keep my toes warm and every time I look down at my green fuzzy
slip-ons, I can't help but take things a little less seriously.

east bay

berkeley, oakland

Priced out of SF rents, a lot of people have been
moving to the East Bay, to the idealistic college
town of Berkeley or edgy Oakland, where small
artsy hoods are popping up downtown and
in Temescal. Berkeley is home to the original
gourmet ghetto, a large cluster of ethnic eats in
casual cafés near the university. It's all very family
friendly and still pretty hippie, a leftover from the
'60s, much like San Francisco's Haight. Oakland,
on the other hand, is more of a checkerboard in
terms of areas that are fun to venture into. So
stick to the pockets I've outlined, and you'll see
why Oakland is becoming a food and shopping
destination again.

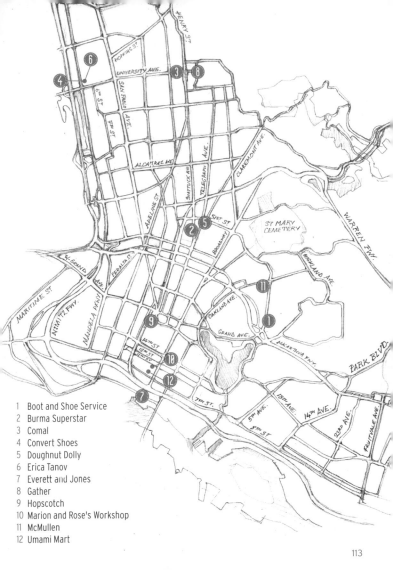

1 Boot and Shoe Service
2 Burma Superstar
3 Comal
4 Convert Shoes
5 Doughnut Dolly
6 Erica Tanov
7 Everett and Jones
8 Gather
9 Hopscotch
10 Marion and Rose's Workshop
11 McMullen
12 Umami Mart

BOOT AND SHOE SERVICE

New American with an egg on top

3308 Grand Avenue / (+1) 510 763 2668 / bootandshoeservice.com
Closed Monday

It was late Sunday morning when a friend suggested we skip the brunch lines in San Francisco and head to Oakland instead. We must have totally stuck out, going through the SF anxiety dance of sending one person to get in line for a table while the driver searched for a parking spot. It turns out that brunch here is much more laid-back than in SF. I was stunned when I rushed into Boot and Shoe Service and was seated immediately despite it being full. Not at the bar (though they have a great one), and not after queuing for two hours. How very civilized. The food is casual new American with an emphasis on eggs and pizza every which way.

BURMA SUPERSTAR

Asian mash-up for the masses

**4721 Telegraph Avenue / (+1) 510 652 2900 / burmasuperstar.com
Open daily**

The food at Burma Superstar is awesome, but, as they openly admit
on their menu, it is heavily influenced by the cuisines of the kingdom's
bordering countries, so it's not wholly authentic Burmese. On my
first visit, I had no idea what to order from the list of 100-something
dishes. After telling me "everything's great", the waiter started to get
impatient (it's a busy place), so a neighboring diner recommended
the eggplant. The waiter gave me a sympathetic look and whispered,
"OK, everything but the eggplant." He then said he'd take care of me,
bringing out a Rainbow Salad and spicy minced lamb. But not before
the other diner had left.

COMAL

Fireside Mexican and margaritas

2020 Shattuck Avenue / (+1) 510 926 6300
comalberkeley.com / Open daily

The streets of downtown Berkeley are lined with awesome little ethnic cafés and take-outs for grub made by someone's grandma. At Comal, three or four sweet-looking señoras stand up front in the open kitchen making hand-pressed tortillas from scratch. Otherwise, this is a very trendy (albeit tasty) take on Mexican in a huge space that could probably fit 20 of its neighboring eateries. I liked sitting in the lively beer garden sipping margaritas and watching people who couldn't get into the dining room dive into tacos at the bar. In my mind, this place is ideal for a late Saturday night snack and last call for mescal.

CONVERT SHOES

Eco-friendly (and cute!) shoes

1844 4th Street / (+1) 510 984 0142 / convertstyle.com / Open daily

In the East Bay, "green" rules the day, often at the expense of style. But you wouldn't know it at Randy Brewer's Convert Shoes, the sister store to his nearby clothing atelier. Randy's team curates a fun roundup of styles for those who care about their ecological footprint. No do-gooder's shop is without clogs, but the ones here are not your mom's brown Birkenstocks. I'm talking metallic high-heeled Maguba clogs from Sweden. Shoemaker Jeffrey Campbell, a friend of Randy's, also did a vegan line for Convert. It's good to walk around in a comfortable pair of T-strap flats that will neither harm my arches nor the planet.

DOUGHNUT DOLLY

Made to order donuts with glorious fillings

482 49th Street / (+1) 510 338 6738 / doughnutdolly.com
Closed Monday and Tuesday

Blink and you'll miss Temescal Alley, a hidden enclave of cool boutiques, cafés and design shops. Probably the best way to spot it is by looking for the line snaking out the door of Doughnut Dolly. Instead of stale, glazed rings on display under your typical 24-hour coffee shop lighting, the gals behind the counter here prepare custom-filled varieties. The choices rotate based on the season, but you can count on crème fraîche, pastry cream, lemon curd and chocolate hazelnut to almost always be on hand. Light, fluffy and not too sweet, these are donuts that take fresh to a whole new level.

ERICA TANOV

Beauty and the boho

1827 4th Street / (+1) 510 849 3331 / ericatanov.com / Open daily

The second I saw a mix of popping florals with paisley and Asian landscape prints in the window, I got excited. Designer Erica Tanov is queen of the clash, somehow making bright prints of all persuasions work together in her very cool clothing and housewares. She gets a lot of her inspiration from her travels, always coming back with new styles to add to her boho chic collection. The store setup is picture perfect too, with gorgeous linens piled in tall stacks against white walls that let the ever-changing merchandise form the patina: a mix of decay, nature and worldly heirlooms. It's enough to make a girl feel giddy.

EVERETT AND JONES

Barbecue rib shack

126 Broadway / (+1) 510 663 2350 / eandjbbq.com / Open daily

The interior of Everett and Jones is a lot like an indoor patio with umbrella-covered picnic tables and big screens showing "live" games. Come Sunday, sports fans are glued to the TVs, while church ladies in fantastic hats and matching dresses sip iced tea. No matter the atmosphere, we were here for the grub. My fellow hunter Meghan gave a sticky thumbs up to the sauce-smothered ribs, spicy greens and cheesy grits. And she's a tough judge, having grown up in Knoxville, Tennessee; a place where everyone is born knowing their way around a barbecue pit.

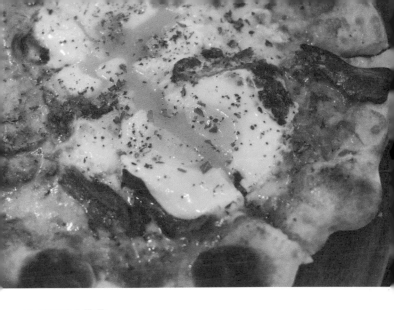

GATHER

Health and harmony

2200 Oxford Street / (+1) 510 809 0400 / gatherrestaurant.com
Open daily

I met Ari Derfel, one of the owners of Gather, when he was leading a backpacking trip in Yosemite. Around the campfire, he told me about his dream for an eco-friendly restaurant, one that was open and spacious, filled with plants and serving up seasonal, organic, elegant comfort food. Ari also wanted to employ troubled teens and teach them how to cook. Two years later, his vision came to life. The cynic in me would usually roll her eyes at all this earnestness, but it's hard to be disparaging when the food's this good: Chef Sean Baker was even named *Esquire*'s 2010 Chef of the Year.

HOPSCOTCH

American diner with a Japanese twist

1915 San Pablo Avenue / (+1) 510 788 6217 / hopscotchoakland.com
Closed Monday

Forget French toast and boring scrambled eggs. On Sunday morning,
I prefer something spicy with rice, a piece of broiled salmon, and
anything glazed with miso. Which is why I adore chef Kyle Itani's
Japanese-influenced weekend menu. His fried rice with Japanese kimchi
is the bomb, and the jidori eggs have that creamy center yolk that I love.
Because it's brunch in a casual-hipster diner setting, coffee's a must,
along with something a little boozy. The best part is that for such a great
brunch spot, there's rarely a wait and street parking is a breeze.

MARION AND
ROSE'S WORKSHOP

Locally made keepsakes

461 9th Street / (+1) 510 214 6794 / marionandrose.com
Closed Monday

Marion and Rose were the names of the grandmothers of both owner Kerri
Johnson and her ex-business partner, but Kerri decided to keep Rose in the
name after her partner moved on. And the moniker makes sense when you
learn that her mission is to harken back to old local stores where you'd buy
things to use for a long time before passing them down to your grandkids.
Kerri is something of a sentimentalist and hand-selects old-timey homeware,
accessories and objets d'art from Bay Area makers to sell in her sunny
boutique. One Friday a month, she keeps the shop open late for a sale.

MCMULLEN

A little luxury in Oak-town

1235 Grand Avenue / (+1) 510 658 6906 / shopmcmullen.com
Open daily

Of all the microhoods in Oakland, Piedmont is my favorite. It's not as young as Temescal and not nearly as stuffy as the hills. No, Piedmont is casual but can step into something elegant when called upon, a lot like Sherri McMullen's boutique up the way from the brunch spots. Peanut, Sherri's Yorkshire terrier, greets customers at the door and leads the way to a rack of long and flowy summer dresses, on-trend flats and timeless blazers. There he leaves you to browse while he finds a sun spot to curl up in for a snooze. Until, of course, it's time to welcome the next person who enters "his" shop.

UMAMI MART

All things Japanese

815 Broadway / (+1) 510 575 9152 / umamimart.com / Closed Monday

You can't help but admire the handpicked barware and stylish kitchen goods Yoko Kumano and Kayoko Akabori import from Tokyo to their elegant shop. My first thought when I walked in was that Umami Mart was like a gorgeous blog or Pinterest board come to life, and then Yoko told me that in fact they began Umami Mart as a blog where they showcased all their favorite stuff. Added to the mix in their offline minimalist store are independent food magazines from all over the world, plus Japanese snacks and drinks that you'd be hard pressed to find anywhere else. No Internet connection required.

flea markets

Your hunting guide for a piece of Bay Area style

ALAMEDA POINT ANTIQUES FAIRE
2900 Navy Way (Alameda), (+1) 510 522 7500,
alamedapointantiquesfaire.com, first Sunday of the month

ALEMANY FLEA MARKET
100 Alemany Boulevard, (+1) 415 647 2043,
facebook.com/pages/Alemany-Flea-Market, every Sunday

TREASURE ISLAND FLEA
1 Avenue of the Palms (Treasure Island), (+1) 415 898 0245,
treasureislandflea.com, last weekend of the month

The list of things that will get me up before dawn is brief. The open-air flea market at the **Alameda Point Antiques Faire** in East Bay on the first Sunday of the month makes the cut though. Diehards and interior designers rise early for the opening of the gates at 6am. Within an hour or two, most of the good stuff – mid-century modern coffee tables, Fiesta ware, vintage record cabinets – is bought up. A couple of other hints: first of all, you've got to haggle. In fact, the sellers expect it and might even be offended if you're not willing to play the game. Just try to play fairly and aim for up to 20% off. Everything is negotiable, compare prices at the hundreds of stalls. Also, bring layers and sunscreen. It's windy and miserable at the start of this open-air market, but come 10am, the sun beats down hard and the fog clears to reveal an amazing view of San Francisco across the bay.

Speaking of which, the bottom of Bernal Hill in SF is home to the **Alemany Flea Market** that takes place every Sunday morning. It is smaller than Alameda by far and has less of an emphasis on bona fide antiques, but the prices are lower and the hunt for treasures can be pretty satisfying. (I found an amazing Bakelite box amongst a heap of old luggage there.)

In between Alemany and Alameda, right in the middle of the Bay Bridge, is the **Treasure Island Flea**. On the last Saturday and Sunday of every month, I like to take a water taxi out to the sprawling market and load up on small antiques, a hot breakfast burrito to warm up, and (later) popsicles to cool off. Out of the three markets, Treasure Island is the most adventurous, and well worth a visit even if you leave empty-handed.

ALAMEDA POINT ANTIQUES FAIRE